Discovering Science

ELECTRICITY
AND
MAGNETISM

Rebecca Hunter

RAINTREE
STECK-VAUGHN
PUBLISHERS

A Harcourt Company

Austin   New York
www.steck-vaughn.com

Published by Raintree Steck-Vaughn Publishers, an imprint of Steck-Vaughn Company.

Acknowledgments
Project Editors: Rebecca Hunter, Pam Wells
Art Director: Max Brinkmann
Illustrated by Joanna Williams, Jenny Mumford, Stefan Chabluk, and Keith Williams
Designed by Ian Winton

Planned and produced by Discovery Books

Library of Congress Cataloging-in-Publication Data
Hunter, Rebecca (Rebecca K. de C.)
Electricity and magnetism / Rebecca Hunter.
p. cm. — (Discovering science)
Includes index.
Summary: Explains how electricity and magnetism are related, how they can be harnessed and how they are useful.
ISBN 0-7398-2970-X (hardcover)
1. Electricity—Juvenile literature. 2. Magnetism—Juvenile literature.
[1. Electricity. 2. Magnetism] I. Title.

QC572.2 .H85 2000
537—dc21

00-028538

1 2 3 4 5 6 7 8 9 0 BNG 04 03 02 01 00
Printed and bound in the United States of America.

Note to the reader: Difficult words are in the glossary in the back of the book.

CONTENTS

OUR ELECTRIC WORLD

BEFORE ELECTRICITY

One hundred and fifty years ago, machines that ran on electricity had not been invented. Houses did not have electric lights. People used candles or gaslights to see in the dark. You could not watch television or listen to a stereo.

Before electricity there were no electric stoves or microwave ovens, so cooking had to be done over an open fire.

There were no electric machines for farming or industry. Businesses depended on work done by hand, steam engines, or water for power. There were no computers and no electronic mail. Letters were written by hand with a pen and ink.

ELECTRICITY TODAY

Electricity is necessary to our lives today. It powers our homes, factories, and schools. It lets us light up the streets at night.

Electricity helps us to communicate, or share ideas and information, with people on the other side of the world instantly.

All computers run on electricity.

CURRENT ELECTRICITY

Electricity is a form of energy. The type of electricity you use most often is called current electricity. This type can flow or move.

Imagine you have a piece of a plastic tube filled with marbles. If you make a circle from the tube and push one of the marbles 1 inch (3 cm), then all the marbles will move just that much around the circle. The power of your push is passed from one marble to the next.

When you turn on an electric switch, the light comes on instantly.

An electric current flows in a similar way to this. It flows through a wire instead of a plastic tube. Instead of marbles, the wire is filled with tiny particles called electrons. Electrons carry an electric charge through the wire. The electrons, like the marbles, do not move very fast, but the electric charge moves at the speed of light. That is 186,000 miles (300,000 km) per second!

▼ *Electricity is carried across the countryside by cables and towers.*

ELECTRIC CIRCUITS

An electric current needs three things to work. First, it needs a path to move along, which is usually a wire. Second, it needs a source of electrical energy. One source of electrical energy is a dry cell, or battery, which stores chemical energy. This energy can be changed to electricity. The third thing that is needed is a circuit for the current to flow around. A circuit is like a circle. Electricity can only flow around a complete circle or circuit. If the circuit is broken, the flow of electricity stops.

This cable car in New Zealand runs on electricity and needs a very large electric motor to make it work.

All electric appliances need a source of electricity. Some things use dry cells for their power. Larger electrical devices must be plugged into an outlet to work.

A hairdryer needs to be plugged into an electric outlet.

PROJECT

Make an electric circuit

You will need
A D-cell battery in a holder
Two pieces of wire
A small lightbulb in a bulb holder

1. Attach one piece of wire to one end of the D-cell and one side of the bulb holder.

2. Attach the other piece of wire to the other end of the D-cell and the other side of the bulb holder.

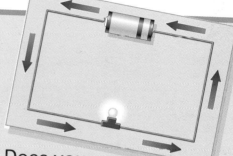

3. Does your bulb light up? If it does, you have made an electric circuit.

4. What happens if you pull one of the wires loose and break the circuit? The bulb goes out because the circuit is no longer complete.

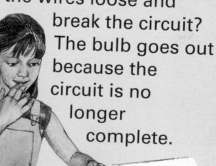

USEFUL ELECTRICITY

Power plant

Electricity towers

Thick wire cable

cable

Current electricity is very useful. It can be switched on and off very quickly. It can be carried along wires to where it is needed. Electrical energy can be changed into forms of other energy, such as light, heat, and mechanical energy. The electricity you use in your home comes from power plants. It is carried from these plants by wires and cables to where it is needed.

Electric current enters your home through a single cable, or bundle of wires. From here wires carry current to every room in the house.

Each room has switches and outlets. We plug all the electric devices that we use each day into these outlets.

In a lightbulb an electric current flows through a thin wire filament. The filament gets so hot that it glows with a bright light.

CONDUCTORS AND INSULATORS

Some materials let electricity flow through them. These are called conductors. Others do not let electricity pass through them. They are called insulators. Conductors provide a path for electricity to follow. Insulators are used to keep electricity from flowing to places where it is not wanted.

An American standard plug

PROJECT

Conductors and insulators.

You will need

A D-cell battery in a holder

Three pieces of wire

A small lightbulb in a bulb holder

Objects made of different materials, such as a coin, a paper clip, an eraser, a key, a plastic pen, a glass bottle, aluminum foil, and cardboard.

1. Make up the electric circuit using three wires as shown.

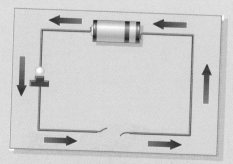

2. Check that it works by touching the two loose wires together.

3. Add each of the objects one after another to the circuit between the two loose wires.

4. Put all the things that let the bulb light up in one pile. These are conductors.

5. Put all the things that do not allow the bulb to light up in another pile. These are insulators.

What do the things in each pile have in common? What are they made of?

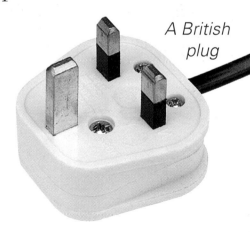

All metals conduct electricity. If they do not, check to see if they are painted or varnished. Plastic and rubber are good insulators. Electric cables, wires, and

An American grounded plug

plugs are covered by plastic or rubber. It is important to make sure these coverings do not become damaged.

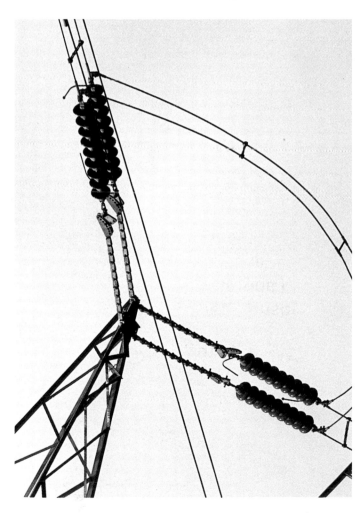

▲ *Porcelain and glass are good insulators and are often used on electricity towers.*

Water is also a good conductor of electricity. Never touch a light switch with wet hands. You could get a really painful shock.

A British plug

A European plug

STATIC ELECTRICITY

One type of electricity does not flow along a current. This is static electricity. Have you ever heard little snapping sounds or seen a spark when you took off your sweater? Have you ever gotten a shock when you touched something metal after walking on a rug? These things are caused by static electricity.

PROJECT

You can charge a balloon with static electricity.

You will need

A woolen sweater
A balloon
A kitchen faucet
Some small pieces of paper or polystyrene

Blow up the balloon, rub it on the woolen sweater to charge it with static electricity. Now try these three quick experiments.

1. Hold the balloon against a wall in a warm, dry room.

2. Hold the balloon near a slow stream of water from a faucet.

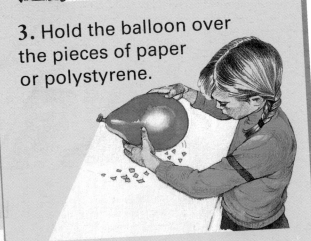

3. Hold the balloon over the pieces of paper or polystyrene.

What happens?
In each case, the balloon attracts the things because of its electric charge.

Static electricity is not very useful. In one way it can be quite dangerous. Lightning is caused by powerful static electricity formed in clouds during thunderstorms. Lightning can cause great harm. Because it usually takes the shortest route to the ground, tall buildings are most likely to be struck by lightning.

To reduce the chance of this happening, many tall buildings have metal rods going down their sides. These are called lightning rods. If lightning strikes the top of the building, the electricity will flow safely down the metal rod to the ground.

AMANING!

AMAZING!
Between 1942 and 1977, a park ranger was struck by lightning seven different times. Amazingly he survived!

MAKING ELECTRICITY

One source of electricity is a generator. You may have a generator on your bike. As the wheels of the bike turn, part of the generator also turns. Then, mechanical energy is changed into electricity by the generator. That electricity can be used to make the lights on your bike work.

Generator

The alternator on a car is also a type of generator. It is turned by the engine. This movement generates the electricity that powers the car's lights, heater, and music system.

Cars would not be able to travel at night without electric lights.

ELECTRIC POWER PLANTS

Most of the electricity we use in our homes, schools, stores, and factories is generated in power plants. Many power plants burn fossil fuels, such as coal or natural gas. The burning heats water to make steam. Moving steam is used to turn a large fan called a turbine. The moving turbine causes parts inside the generator to move and generate electricity.

Electricity is generated using nuclear power at this power plant in Ontario, Canada.

ELECTRICITY FROM WATER

Electricity can be generated from moving water, too. Hydroelectric power (HEP) plants use moving water to turn their turbines. HEP plants are often built in countries that have high rainfall and mountains with fast flowing streams. Countries like Canada, Sweden, Scotland, and the United States use HEP. One-fourth of the world's electricity is produced this way.

This power plant produces hydroelectric power from the water behind the Shasta Dam in Redding, California.

ELECTRICITY FROM WIND

The power of the wind can also generate electricity. In California, one wind farm has 300 wind turbines that supply electricity to the area around Los Angeles.

These wind turbines are part of a wind farm in California.

ELECTRICITY FROM THE SUN

The Sun is also an important energy source. Energy from the Sun is called solar energy. The Sun's energy can be converted, or changed, into electricity inside something called solar cells. This type of energy is useful. It is a clean source of energy, and one that will not run out like other natural resources.

MAGNETISM

WHAT IS MAGNETISM?

Magnetism is the ability of a piece of metal or rock to attract something to it or to repel, or push away, certain materials.

Magnets can make things move without actually touching them.

Bar magnet

Ring magnet

Horseshoe magnet

Most magnets are made from iron or steel and can be made into many different shapes.

You can make amazing sculptures with these magnetized shapes.

What Will a Magnet Attract?

The most magnetic material is pure iron. However, iron is rarely found in its pure form. It is usually mixed with other metals. Anything that has iron in it will be somewhat magnetic.

PROJECT

Try testing some objects to find out which ones are magnetic.

You will need

A strong magnet

A group of objects to be tested: a paper clip, a coin, aluminum foil, an eraser, a pencil, a plastic bottle cap, a china mug, a spoon, a leaf

1. Sort the objects into two groups. One group will be those that you think will be magnetic. The other will be those you think won't be.

2. Now test each group by holding the magnet over each object. If the object is drawn to the magnet, it is magnetic.

3. Write a list of the objects that are magnetic and another of those that are not.

Did you guess correctly? What does this tell you about some of the metals you tested?

MAGNETIC POLES

The ends of a magnet are called poles. Each magnet has a North and a South pole. Magnets are often labeled. The North pole is labeled N, and the South pole is labeled S. Sometimes magnets are painted so that the North pole is red and the South pole is blue.

A North pole will always be attracted to the South pole of another magnet. Two South poles will repel, or push away from, each other. The same thing would take place with two North poles.

PROJECT

Magnetic poles

You will need

Two bar magnets
Two toy plastic cars
A clear strip of tape for fastening

1. Tape a magnet to the roof of each toy car with the two North poles at the front of both cars.

2. If you roll the cars toward each other, the two North poles will repel each other. Then, the cars will be pushed apart.

3. If you move one car up behind the other, the North and South poles will attract each other. Then, you will have caused a crash!

MAGNETIC FIELDS

The push or pull of a magnet is called its magnetic force. Most of the force of a magnet is at its ends. However, the force spreads in all directions along the magnet. This space around a magnet, in which the magnetic force is felt, is called the magnetic field.

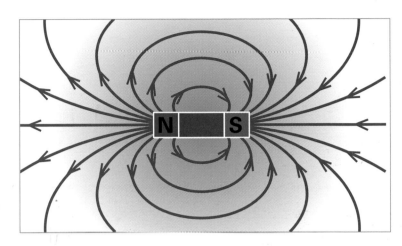

PROJECT

Look at a magnet's lines of force.

You will need

A bar magnet
Some iron filings, or shavings
A thin sheet of plastic or piece of paper

1. Place the sheet of plastic or piece of paper over the magnet.

2. Shake the iron filings gently over the area where the magnet is.

3. Look at the pattern made by the iron filings.

MAKING MAGNETS

Some metals can be made into magnets.
Try making a magnet.

PROJECT

You will need
A strong bar magnet
A long steel nail
Some paper clips

1. First, test to see if the nail is magnetic. Does it attract the paper clips?

2. Hold the nail on the table with one hand. Use your other hand to stroke the nail with the magnet. Always stroke it with the same end of the magnet and always move the magnet down the nail in the same direction.

3. Stroke it about 30 times. Now, see if it is magnetic. How many paper clips can it pick up? Try stroking it again. See if you can make it more magnetic. Will it pick up more paper clips?

HOW DOES THIS WORK?

A magnetic material can be thought of as holding millions of tiny magnets. In a magnet, these tiny magnets all face the same way. In a material that is not magnetic, these magnets face in different directions.

By stroking the steel nail with a magnet, you started to line up the tiny magnets inside the nail in one direction. With each stroke of the magnet, some of the tiny magnets were pulled into line. The more you stroked, the more tiny magnets were lined up. The nail became a stronger magnet.

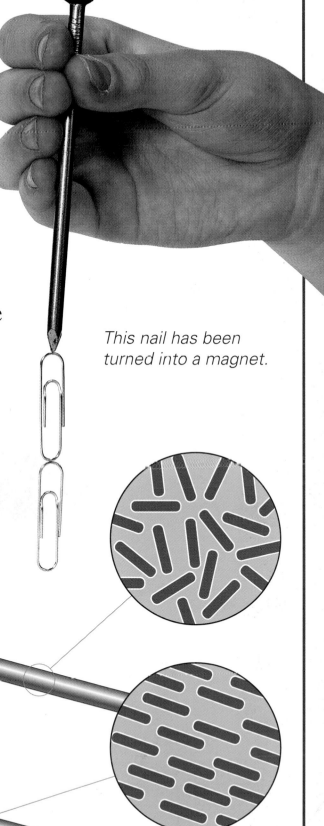

This nail has been turned into a magnet.

Nonmagnetic nail

Magnetic nail

EARTH AS A MAGNET

Earth acts as if it had a huge bar magnet inside it. This is caused by the very hot, iron core at the center of Earth. If there were a bar magnet inside our planet, it would have one end at the magnetic North pole. The other end would be at the magnetic South pole. Remember that the magnetic poles are not quite the same as Earth's geographic North and South poles.

Earth behaves like a giant magnet.

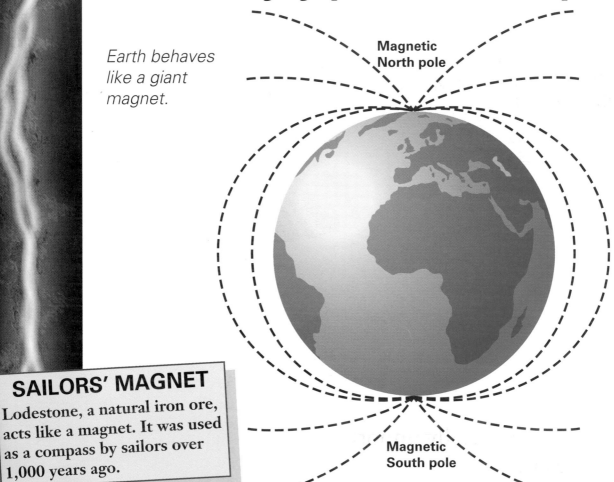

Magnetic North pole

Magnetic South pole

SAILORS' MAGNET
Lodestone, a natural iron ore, acts like a magnet. It was used as a compass by sailors over 1,000 years ago.

Lines of magnetic force run through Earth from one pole to the other. If it is allowed to turn freely, a magnet will align itself with the magnetic North and South poles. This is what makes a compass work.

PROJECT

Make a compass

You will need
A large needle
A small piece of cork or polystyrene
A magnet
A saucer of water

1. First, you need to make the needle act like a magnet. You do this by stroking it with a magnet. Do this at least 20 times.

2. Now, lay the needle on the piece of cork or polystyrene.

3. Float it in the dish of water.

The needle will swing around to point in a North-South direction. This is what a real compass does.

A compass is especially important in helping ships at sea to find their way. Many drivers and hikers use compasses to guide them.

ELECTROMAGNETISM

MAGNETISM AND ELECTRICITY

Magnetism and electricity are closely related. There are magnets in the generators that produce electricity. There are also magnets inside electric motors. An electric current can produce its own magnetic field. Electricity can also be used to create a magnet. Such magnets are called electromagnets.

PROJECT

Make an electromagnet.

You will need
A D-cell battery in a holder
A long iron nail
Some plastic covered wire [about 2-3 feet (60-100cm)]
Some paper clips or pins

1. Wind the wire around the nail about ten times.

2. Attach one end of the wire to one terminal, or the connection point on the battery. Attach the other end to the other terminal.

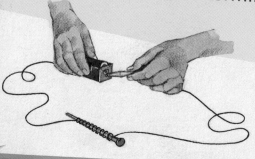

3. Hold the nail over the paper clips or pins. What happens?

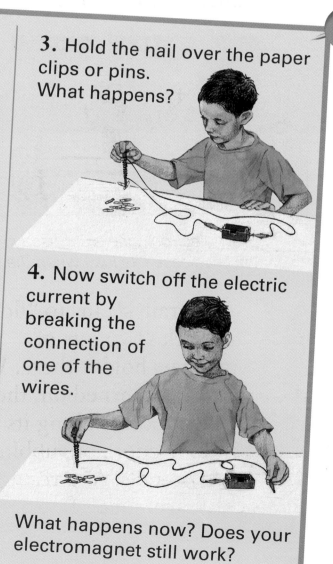

4. Now switch off the electric current by breaking the connection of one of the wires.

What happens now? Does your electromagnet still work?

The electricity flowing through the tight coils of wire creates a strong magnetic field from one end of the coil to the other. The force lines up all the magnetic particles in the nail and turns it into a magnet. The more coils of wire there are, the stronger the magnetic force.

Electromagnets are very useful because the magnetism can be switched on and off with the electricity. Electromagnets are found in many things in a house, such as televisions, telephones, and doorbells.

Very strong electromagnets are used in junkyards to sort scrap metal. The magnet releases its load when the electric current is switched off.

A magnetic train seems to "float" above its track. Two sets of electromagnets hold it there. When the electricity is turned on, the train glides very smoothly along its track. There is no friction, or rubbing, of the wheels on rails. As a result, these trains can travel much faster than ordinary trains. The train stops when the electricity is turned off.

GLOSSARY

alternator An electric generator that produces an electric current.

circuit A path around which electricity can flow.

conductor A substance that allows electricity to flow through it.

current The flow of electrons through a wire.

electromagnet A magnet made by passing electricity through a wire wrapped around an iron core.

electron A negatively charged particle.

generator A device that converts mechanical energy into electricity.

grounded Today, most electrical sockets have three wires. Two wires carry the current, and the third wire, the ground wire, is for safety. If there is a buildup of electrical charge, the ground wire carries the charge safely to the ground.

hydroelectric power Electricity produced by the movement of water.

insulator A material that does not allow electricity to pass through it.

magnetic field The space near a magnet where magnetic power can be noticed.

magnetic poles The two points on a magnet where the magnetic effect is strongest.

magnetism An invisible force between substances.

turbine A machine that is made to rotate to drive a generator.

FURTHER READING

Baker, Wendy, and others. *Electricity* (Make It Work? Eureka! Series). Scholastic.

Challand, Helen J. *Experiments with Electricity*. Childrens, 1986.

DePinna, Simon. *Electricity* (Science Projects series). Raintree Steck-Vaughn, 1998.

Madgwick, Wendy. *Magnets and Sparks* (Science Starters series). Raintree Steck-Vaughn, 1999.

Parker, Steve. *Thomas Edison and Electricity* (Science Discoveries series). Harper Collins Child Books, 1992.

Riley, Peter. *Electricity and Magnetism* (Smart Science series). Heinemann Library, 1999.

The publishers would like to thank the following for permission to reproduce their pictures:

Beamish Museum: page 4; **Chris Fairclough**: page 7, 13; **Discovery Picture Library**: page 9, top, 20, 25, 27; **Science Photo Library**: page 15, (Kent Wood), 18, (John Mead), 19, (Russel D Curtis), 29, (Alex Bartel); **gettyone Stone**: page 5 top (Cosmo Condina), bottom (David Young Wolff), 9, bottom (Doug Armand), 11 (Paul Dance), 16, (Ken Biggs), 17, (John Edwards).

INDEX